A book about Howard Gardner's Theory

Written by Mary R. Massey, Ed.D.

Illustrated by April Bensch

All rights reserved. No part of this book may be reproduced, stored in a retrieval system, or transmitted by any means—electronic, mechanical, photocopying, recording, or otherwise—without the written permission of the publisher.

Copyright © 2017 Mary R. Massey

All rights reserved.

ISBN-13: 978-1547102266
ISBN-10: 1547102268

Foreword

Educators that are sensitive to children's needs assist them in becoming more physically fit, active, well-coordinated and adjusted. Physical, social, emotional, creative and mental skills can be enhanced through careful planning of the curriculum and the classroom environment. The classroom environment is a primary motivating force for a young child's self-concept, determining the way he or she feels about her- or himself and others.

Children can lengthen their attention span, increase personal rapport between adults and peers, reduce tension, establish a 'success syndrome' and enhance academic readiness and intellectual potential when appropriate teaching methods are utilized. The way a child sees his or her body and the ability to successfully perform tasks influences several aspects of affective (emotional-social) development. An educator's goal is for every child to participate successfully in a variety of activities that promote their maximum development.

As Mary's university professor, I saw her enhance our classes with her knowledge of learning modality principles and how to implement special educational strategies to engage all children in active learning. Her enthusiasm, compassion and experiences continue to foster successful learning for every individual child. Mary is truly one of education's BEST teachers; she is definitely 'Kid Smart', applying and sharing her valuable research in effective, innovative ways!

Elaine Van Lue, Ed.D.
Professor, Nova Southeastern University
Orlando, Florida
June 2017

DEDICATION

This book is dedicated to my son, William, on whom the character **Will, the Word SMART Wizard** is based. Will has always been intrigued by words and word play, even as a young child. He spoke very early as an infant/toddler and I believe that is, in part, because I was a public school music teacher the entire 40 weeks he was in utero. The environment was filled with language for him to absorb naturally. Additionally, he grew up watching Mr. Roger's Neighborhood and Sesame Street, which contributed greatly to his extensive vocabulary and love for words. Will's musical/rhythmic intelligence, or Music SMART abilities, developed early as well, because of this constant exposure to music and sounds before and after his birth. Genetics may have played a part, as well! It has been a joy and a great sense of pride to witness Will's growth and development into adulthood.

ACKNOWLEDGMENTS

I am grateful for my daughter, Alexandra, who serves as the Editor for my books. She not only worked on the formatting and layout for this book, but she offered several suggestions that enhanced the outcome of the story. Once again, her insight and understanding of Gardner's theory have allowed her to be an incredible resource for me. Her deep level of creativity continues to astound me and I am so grateful she is willing to ride this writer's rollercoaster with me! It doesn't hurt that she knows her big brother very well, either! Take note, the reader will see a glimpse into Alex and her SMARTEST PART in **Alex, the Music SMART Maestro** as we watch Alexandra spread her wings and soar in the third book of my SMART Parts series. Alex's book will focus on the musical/rhythmic intelligence, Alex's Music SMART Part.

WILL
The Word SMART Wizard

Book #2 in my SMART Parts series focuses on Will and Word SMART. It shows how Will uses this dominant intelligence to work on developing some of his other SMART parts. It's important to remember we *all* are born with *every* SMART part and we have the ability to develop them to their full potential. Isn't that great news!?!? The character of **Will, the Word SMART Wizard** is modeled after my son, Will. He is definitely Word SMART and has a great time sharing jokes, puns, riddles, and funny stories. Will is also an accomplished presenter. He is a Regional HR Manager with a national golf management company and is called upon regularly to present information to staff and train new staff members. I've seen video of some of Will's presentations and they are quite entertaining! His command of the English language gives him a wonderful advantage in communicating with others, whether it be for official presentations or in familiar conversation. Will loves to play basketball, golf, rollerblade, and water ski, which are wonderful ways to strengthen his Body SMART part! Will's Music SMART part is highly developed as is evident by the fact that he plays several instruments and has an incredible bass singing voice. Will is a loyal fan of the University of Florida Gators, his Alma Mater, and his beloved Chicago Cubs! April's illustration of Will is modeled from his "bowl cut" days. It is a very accurate depiction of him, as you can see in the real-life picture of Will as a child. He chattered away as a baby and toddler, talking and singing throughout his day, every day. Yes, Will is truly Word SMART. The two new characters introduced in this book are modeled after Will's wife, Natalie, and their dog, Macallan.

One bright morning, a group of friends ran to the field where the old road ends.

Will was thrilled to play ball with his pals.

He has a lot in common with these guys and gals.

They all love to have fun and do things together.

Learning about SMART parts has only made them better.

Will is word SMART and all
his friends can see
he is a *Word SMART Wizard*
with a huge vocabulary.

Whirling words of wonder start Will's day with lots of fun.

His mind is busy thinking of a silly baseball pun.

His friends began to chuckle and Will felt ten feet tall.

Will's clever words and jokes are always a big hit.

His friends all stop and think, then laugh when they finally 'get it'!

Being word SMART helps Will in many different ways.
Sad times seem much easier with puns, jokes, and word plays.

Or when he met Natalie,
his new friend,
and didn't know what to say,
he quickly made up a rhyme and
his fears melted away.

When Will saw Alex sad and wanted to cheer her up, he told her a funny joke about Macallan, his sweet little pup.

"What did Macallan say to the tree?"
Will asked his little friend.
"I'm not sure," Alex replied.
"He said, 'BARK!'" Will said with a grin.

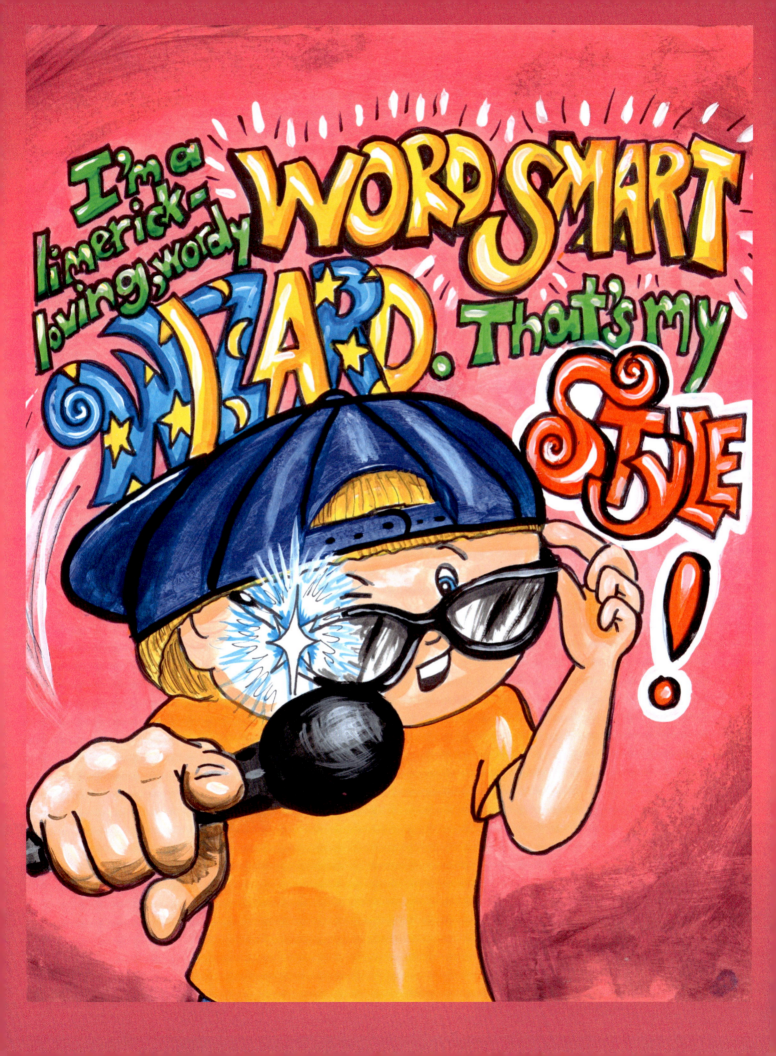

...so he can strengthen other SMART parts each and every day.

By tapping into all the other SMART parts that are his,

Will can use his love of words to be the WIZ he is!

Many words and phrases play a part in Will's word fun...

...but nothing beats the sound of hearing his friends shout, "HOMERUN!"

THE END

Or maybe it's just the beginning of your SMART PARTS discovery!

WORD SMART RAP
Lyrics by Mary R. Massey

I'm a rapper who is dapper!
I'm a word SMART kind of guy!
I deliver jokes and puns
And have a lot of fun, here's why:
I love to twist a word or
Turn a phrase to make you smile.
I'm a limerick-loving,
Wordy Word SMART Wizard.
That's my style!

You can hear the "Word SMART Rap" and jam along at
www.hugthemountain.com.

HOW AM I SMART?
Music and Lyrics by Mary R. Massey

How am I SMART?
Which are my "SMART PARTS"?
How am I SMART?
How can I know?
Where do I start
learning my "SMART PARTS"?
How do I start helping them grow?

You can hear the "SMART PARTS" song and sing along at
www.hugthemountain.com.

Visual/Spatial Intelligence
Ellie Rae
ART SMART

Interpersonal Intelligence
Emme
PEOPLE SMART

Body/Kinesthetic Intelligence
Landry
BODY SMART

Logical/Mathematical Intelligence
Lee
NUMBER SMART

SMART

Musical/Rhythmic Intelligence
Alex
MUSIC SMART

Verbal/Linguistic Intelligence
Will
WORD SMART

Intrapersonal Intelligence
Maggie
SELF SMART

Naturalist Intelligence
Jimmy
NATURE SMART

PARTS

Author

Dr. Mary Massey is a lifelong learner who believes all children are SMART, they're just SMART in different ways! She has researched Howard Gardner's *Theory of Multiple Intelligences* (MI) and uses it as a foundation for instruction, as a college professor. She also designs and conducts MI professional development programs for teachers. Mary was raised in South Bend, IN, moved to Foley, AL in high school and is an alumna of Troy (State) University (BME), Troy, AL and Nova Southeastern University (MS & EdD), Fort Lauderdale, FL. She now lives in Tallahassee, Florida with George, her husband of 38 years. She is the Mama of two adult children, William (wife, Natalie) and Alexandra and the Nana of two adorable granddogs, Macallan and Sadie Mae. Keep a lookout for the next book in the SMART Parts series! You can follow Mary on Facebook or read her blog at www.hugthemountain.com.

April Bensch grew up in Tampa, Florida where she developed a deep appreciation for the visual and performing arts. However, she now calls the small town of Pawleys Island, South Carolina home, along with her husband and three beautiful daughters who make up an all-girl band called 3 Nails. April is an award winning artist, published author, art instructor, and illustrator of many publications for people of all ages, but children's books are her absolute favorite. Her other previous artistic works include set design and creation for Word of Life Productions (creators of films such as Fireproof and Face the Giants) as well as a Barry Levinson film (producer of Rain Man and Wag the Dog). She also enjoys rollerblading, gardening, and singing in her church choir. She does not water ski, speak French, or iron. Her artwork can be viewed at www.aprilbensch.com or on Facebook.

Illustrator

PROPERTY OF MURRELL LIBRARY
MISSOURI VALLEY COLLEGE
MARSHALL, MO 65340

DATE DUE

| Feb 22 2023 | |

Made in the USA
Lexington, KY
17 October 2017